D0933717

CLAYTON COMMUNITY LIBRARY FOUNDATION

GIFT OF THE
CLAYTON COMMUNITY
LIBRARY FOUNDATION

Pebble™ Plus

Mighty Machines

Tow Trucks

by Terri DeGezelle

Consulting Editor: Gail Saunders-Smith, PhD

Consultant: Jeff Hunter
Executive Director
California Tow Truck Association

WITHDRAWN

Capstone press

Mankato, Minnesota

Pebble Plus is published by Capstone Press,
151 Good Counsel Drive, P.O. Box 669, Mankato, Minnesota 56002.
www.capstonepub.com

Copyright © 2006 by Capstone Press, a Capstone imprint. All rights reserved.
No part of this publication may be reproduced in whole or in part, or stored in a retrieval system, or transmitted in any form or by any means, electronic, mechanical, photocopying, recording, or otherwise, without written permission of the publisher. For information regarding permission, write to Capstone Press,
151 Good Counsel Drive, P.O. Box 669, Dept. R, Mankato, Minnesota 56002.

Books published by Capstone Press are manufactured with paper containing at least 10 percent post-consumer waste.

Library of Congress Cataloging-in-Publication Data
DeGezelle, Terri, 1955–
Tow trucks / by Terri DeGezelle.
p. cm.—(Pebble plus. Mighty machines)
Summary: "Simple text and photographs present tow trucks, their parts, and their jobs"—Provided by publisher.
Includes bibliographical references and index.
ISBN-13: 978-0-7368-5359-0 (hardcover)
ISBN-10: 0-7368-5359-6 (hardcover)
ISBN-13: 978-0-7368-6908-9 (softcover pbk.)
ISBN-10: 0-7368-6908-5 (softcover pbk.)
1. Wreckers (Vehicles)—Juvenile literature. 2. Automobiles—Towing—Juvenile literature. I. Title. II. Series.
TL230.5.W74D44 2006
629.225—dc22 2005021608

Editorial Credits
Martha E. H. Rustad, editor; Molly Nei, set designer; Ted Williams, book designer; Wanda Winch, photo researcher; Scott Thoms, photo editor

Photo Credits
Capstone Press/Karon Dubke, cover, 1, 4–5, 7, 9, 10–11, 15, 20–21; Landov LLC/Reuters/Hart Matthews, 18-19; Peter Arnold, Inc./Hartmut Schwarzbach, 17; UNICORN Stock Photos/Mark E. Gibson, 12–13

The author thanks Dick Longenecker, Heavy Equipment Operator, Local Union 49er, for his assistance with this book. Pebble Plus thanks All American Towing of Mankato, Minnesota for assistance with photo shoots.

Note to Parents and Teachers

The Mighty Machines set supports national standards related to science, technology, and society. This book describes and illustrates tow trucks. The images support early readers in understanding the text. The repetition of words and phrases helps early readers learn new words. This book also introduces early readers to subject-specific vocabulary words, which are defined in the Glossary section. Early readers may need assistance to read some words and to use the Table of Contents, Glossary, Read More, Internet Sites, and Index sections of the book.

Printed in the United States of America in North Mankato, Minnesota.
112010
005987R

Table of Contents

A Tow Truck's Job 4
Parts of Tow Trucks. 6
What Tow Trucks Do. 14
Mighty Tow Trucks. 20

Glossary 22
Read More 23
Internet Sites. 23
Index 24

A Tow Truck's Job

Tow trucks move
broken cars.
Tow trucks pull cars
to repair shops to be fixed.

5
24HR. EMERGENCY
TOWING
F-350
ALL AMERICAN
TOWING
JERR-DAN
USDOT. 270822
GENERAL
AMERITRAC TW

Parts of Tow Trucks

Tow trucks have radios.
A call on the radio tells
a tow truck driver
where help is needed.

radio

Tow trucks have
lights that flash.
The lights warn
other drivers to be careful
around tow trucks.

lights
ALL AMERICAN
TOWING
5
F-350
SUPER DUTY
24HR. EMERGENCY
TOWING
RR-DAN
SDOT. 270822

Tow trucks have wheel lifts.
The wheel lift raises
the front wheels
of a broken car.

wheel lift

Tow trucks have booms
that stretch out.
Booms help lift big trucks
that have tipped over.

boom
THERMO KING

What Tow Trucks Do

Tow trucks carry tools
for changing tires
and fixing cars.

JERRDAN
10,000 PSI

Tow trucks move broken cars
off the road.
Then traffic can pass by
on the road.

POLIZEI
AUTO BAUER
AUTO BAUER
ADAC
WIS LU 50
HWI HX 94

Tow trucks pull
all kinds of vehicles.
They even tow big trucks.

U.A.M.
492

Mighty Tow Trucks

Tow trucks help people
with broken cars.
Tow trucks are
mighty machines.

MINNESOTA
YS5765G
JERR-DAN
USDOT. 270822
RANGER
XLT
VISION GTS
EL DORADO

Glossary

boom—a long metal arm that sticks out from a tow truck

flash—to blink on and off

radio—a tool, similar to a walkie-talkie, used to send and receive messages

tow—to pull something

traffic—cars and trucks moving along a road

warn—to tell people about danger

wheel lift—a metal bar on a tow truck that is shaped like the letter T; a wheel lift fits under a car's wheels and lifts them up.

Read More

Schaefer, Lola M. *Tow Trucks.* Bridgestone Books: The Transportation Library. Mankato, Minn.: Capstone Press, 2000.

Steele, Michael Anthony. *I'm a Great Big Tow Truck!* New York: Scholastic, 2003.

Internet Sites

FactHound offers a safe, fun way to find Internet sites related to this book. All of the sites on FactHound have been researched by our staff.

Here's how:

1. Visit *www.facthound.com*
2. Type in this special code **0736853596** for age-appropriate sites. Or enter a search word related to this book for a more general search.
3. Click on the **Fetch It** button.

FactHound will fetch the best sites for you!

Index

booms, 12
cars, 4, 10, 14, 16, 20
drivers, 6, 8
fix, 4, 14
lights, 8
radios, 6
repair shops, 4
road, 16
tires, 14
tools, 14
traffic, 16
wheel lifts, 10

Word Count: 132
Grade: 1
Early-Intervention Level: 16